LET'S PLAY!

WITHDRAWN
...e County Library

Jump, jump with a rope, skip, skip as high as you can. Can you jump with a rope like these Africans?

Back and forth these two Indian children go. A swing is great fun, but it's more fun with two.

'Clink!' go the marbles as they bump together. 'Splash!' go the marbles as they land in the puddles; but these **Burmese** boys don't mind!

Hop, jump, hop, jump. In the United Kingdom hopscotch is perfect for the school playground.

Swing, swing from the rings, swing like a gymnast as high as you can! Can you swing like this Chinese girl?

Wiggling his body round and round the Kenyan boy keeps the hoop spinning – he's got to keep going, he can't stop!

Slip, slide over the bumps. These children in America slide all the way down.

Round and round spin the tops. The Japanese children won't let them drop.

One bendy boomerang flying through the air; one young
Australian catching it with care.

Bright red sails on the toy boat, bobbing up and down on the Madagascan Sea.

This big, beautiful butterfly is actually a kite. An Indonesian family take the kite out for a flight.

Bubbles, bubbles in the air, bubble, bubbles fly everywhere.
These Thai children are blowing beautiful bubbles.

Sri Lankan boys are playing football. Kick, pass, shoot, GOAL!

Over the net, over the net, hit the ball back over the net.
These Kenyan boys love playing volleyball.

Giddy up horsey, trot along! A tree and some imagination mean hours of fun in Namibia.

Which way out? Let's run and see. These American children are playing in a maze.

Take one plank and add some wheels – hey presto – you've got a go-kart. Beep beep, make way for these Brazilian boys!

Bend the wire, carefully, carefully. Wrap it around nice and tight. Can you make a car like this clever Namibian boy?

'Roar!' goes the polar bear, but don't be afraid – this Russian bear is made from snow!

'Whoosh!' goes the sledge. 'Wheee!' go the children. Sledging in Europe is really good fun.

Some games are quiet like this Chinese board game. Shhh. They are trying to think!

Flick the disk into the centre – the closest to the middle wins. Which of these Tanzanian children do you think will get the prize?

Watch out Dad, your boy's going to win! In Malawi a family play this traditional game.

A game of cards with friends can pass the time for hours — especially if the weather's nice like in sunny Brazil.

Going up, coming down, turning round and round.
Have you been on a big wheel like these Indian
children?

Hold on tight, the ride's about to begin. These Nepalese children go for a spin.

The day is at an end, time to tidy away. This European toddler packs his blocks for another day.